I Can Pray Like That?

Like That?

A Prayer Journal for Kids

Written by Colleen Clabaugh

For more information visit our website at:
kidsprayer.com
or
wnop.org

Kids Prayer is a ministry of
World Network of Prayer
8855 Dunn Road, Hazelwood, MO 63042

Each page is filled with random, fun ideas for kids prayer time. The journal includes hands-on activities for praying about things in much different ways than you may have done before.

Instructions for use:

1. Complete the activity on each page.

2. At the bottom of each page are category boxes. Select which one of the categories the prayer activity was related to. For example, if it was a prayer for you, select "Myself." If it was a prayer for a nation, select "My World."

3. Have fun praying, and exploring your life with God and your world in a new way!

When you are done, be sure to send pictures of your journal to:

kidsprayer@wnop.org

We'd love to show off your work!

WRITE IN THE DARK

Use a flashlight to write in your journal today. Think about all of the people in the world who have never heard about Jesus or His love. Think about those who believe in false religions, like Muslims, Buddhists, Communists, Atheists, and Tribal people. They are in **"spiritually dark"** places. Pray for God to send people to them to share the Gospel—**God's Light**. Write your prayer below.

Mark 16:15. And then he told them, "Go into all the world and preach the Good News to everyone.

☐ Myself
☐ My family
☐ My church
☐ My community
☐ My world

So Sleeeppyyy

People worry about a lot of problems. Sometimes they worry so much that they can't sleep well. Think about what things people in our world worry most about, and then write a prayer below for **God's peace** in their lives.

☐ Myself
☐ My family
☐ My church
☐ My community
☐ My world

2 Tim. 1:7. For God hath not given us the spirit of fear; but of power, and of love, and of a sound mind.

kidsprayer.com

YAKITY YAK!

Some people do ALL the talking when it comes to prayer. **Prayer is supposed to be talking to God AND listening to Him too**. If you do all the talking, God can't tell you anything. Take a few minutes and **ask God to talk to you** today. Write down what He tells you below.

Deuteronomy 13:18. The LORD your God will be merciful only if you listen to his voice and keep all his commands that I am giving you today, doing what pleases him.

- ☐ Myself
- ☐ My family
- ☐ My church
- ☐ My community
- ☐ My world

FILL IT WITH DOTS

FILL THIS ENTIRE PAGE WITH TINY DOTS. AS YOU DO, PRAY FOR PATIENCE.

☐ Myself
☐ My family
☐ My church
☐ My community
☐ My world

Galatians 5:22. But the Holy Spirit produces this kind of fruit in our lives: love, joy, peace, patience, kindness, goodness, faithfulness.

!! Breaking News !!

God wants us to pray for the **needs of the world**, not just our own. Paste a **current event** from a newspaper, magazine, or website (with your parents approval).
Write a prayer about the issue.

EXTRA! EXTRA! PRAY ALL ABOUT IT!

Mark 13:8. Nation will go to war against nation, and kingdom against kingdom. There will be earthquakes in many parts of the world, as well as famines.

- ☐ Myself
- ☐ My family
- ☐ My church
- ☐ My community
- ☐ My world

BLOT IT OUT!

The Bible says that everyone has done wrong. Write down below something you have done wrong, or something you should have done, but did not do. Talk to God about it. Ask Him to forgive you and help you know how to change. Using a color, ink pen, pain, mud, coffee grounds, or anything dark, mark it out where you can no longer read it. **Thank God for His forgiveness.**

☐ Myself
☐ My family
☐ My church
☐ My community
☐ My world

1 John 1:9 If we confess our sins, he is faithful and just to forgive us our sins, and to cleanse us from all

kidsprayer.com

Click It!

Jesus told us to love our neighbors, and to be concerned about other people's problems. Take a picture with someone in your **neighborhood** who is not a part of your family. (with your parent's permission) Ask them what you can **pray for them** about, and then do it. If you can print your picture, paste it below.

Matthew 19:19 ...honor your father and mother, and love your neighbor as yourself.

☐ Myself
☐ My family
☐ My church
☐ My community
☐ My world

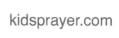
kidsprayer.com

MACARONI MEALS

Poor people in some nations may only get a few meals a week, and then it may be just a little rice or beans. Glue uncooked macaroni noodles below. (Make a picture if you wish.) Pray for those in **poor nations** and those in your areas who need food, clothing, shelter, or a job.

☐ Myself
☐ My family
☐ My church
☐ My community
☐ My world

Proverbs 21:13 Whoso stoppeth his ears at the cry of the poor, he also shall cry himself, but shall not be heard.

PRAYING IN CODE

The Bible tells us that we can't hide anything from God; He knows all of our secrets. Write a prayer below using a **secret** code that you make up on your own. Write the code answers on another page in case you forget what it is. **Share your prayer** with a friend and see if they can figure it out. Pray the prayer together, and pray that you would not hide anything from God but always be **truthful and honest.**

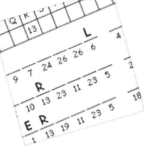

Luke 8:17 *There is nothing hidden that will not be revealed, and there is nothing secret that will not become known and come to light.*

☐ Myself
☐ My family
☐ My church
☐ My community
☐ My world

TAKING TERRITORY

Jesus told us to reach the whole world, and share the gospel with all nations. Use the bottom of your shoe and leave a dirty foot print on the page. Pray that everywhere you, your family, or your church goes, that you will be a **good witness** and **share the gospel**.

☐ Myself
☐ My family
☐ My church
☐ My community
☐ My world

Deuteronomy 11:24 Every place whereon the soles of your feet shall tread shall be yours...

Unplug Those Ears!

Sometimes games, phones, videos, music or friends can take our attention away from praying and being able to listen to God who wants to talk with us. Tape or glue Q-Tips below in the form of a cross. Ask God to help you **listen** and hear Him speaking to you. Ask Him to help you listen to good things, not bad. Write down what **God speaks to you**.

1 Samuel 3:10 Then the LORD came and stood and called as at other times, "Samuel! Samuel!" And Samuel said, "Speak, for Your servant is listening.

☐ Myself
☐ My family
☐ My church
☐ My community
☐ My world

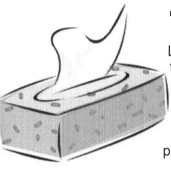

Tears... But No Fears!

Life is difficult at times and it can be hard to deal with. Sometimes problems make people cry or be emotional. Tape someone's tissue below that they used when they cried. Pray that God would **comfort** and help them through their problems. Write their name below and any prayer requests they may have.

- ☐ Myself
- ☐ My family
- ☐ My church
- ☐ My community
- ☐ My world

Psalm 55:22 Give your burdens to the LORD, and he will take care of you.

GIVE IT AWAY!

Change you world! Take some of the allowance you earn one week, or some of the money you earn for doing a job, and tape it below. Ask God what He wants you to do with it to **help someone else**, then do it. Once you have used the money for God's purpose, write down what you did with it below.

2 Corinthians 9:11 You must each decide in your heart how much to give. And don't give reluctantly or in response to pressure. "For God loves a person who gives cheerfully."

- ☐ Myself
- ☐ My family
- ☐ My church
- ☐ My community
- ☐ My world

kidsprayer.com

Have someone else, such as a parent, teacher, pastor, or friend, write a prayer idea below, then do it!

☐ Myself
☐ My family
☐ My church
☐ My community
☐ My world

scripture goes here:

Hair Care

People with cancer often have to have chemotherapy treatments which can make their hair fall out. Find pieces of hair (the more the better) from your comb or sink, and tape them below. Pray for healing for those who have **cancer**.

- ☐ Myself
- ☐ My family
- ☐ My church
- ☐ My community
- ☐ My world

Jeremiah 30:17 For I will restore health unto you, and I will heal you of your wounds, saith the Lord.

PRESIDENTIAL PRAYER

URGENT!

The Bible says that we are to pray for our leaders. Leaders have tough jobs with a lot of responsibility.

Write a letter and a prayer to the **President or leader** of your nation. Paste it below. Make another copy on a piece of paper and ask an adult to help you mail it to the leader. Pray for them.

☐ Myself
☐ My family
☐ My church
☐ My community
☐ My world

1 Timothy 2:1-2 ...I urge you to offer to God petitions, prayers, intercessions, and expressions of thanks for all people, for kings, and for everyone who has authority, so that we might lead a quiet and peaceful life with all godliness and dignity.

kidsprayer.com

STUCK ON BAND-AIDS

God gave us power through His Spirit to pray for those who are sick so they can be **healed**. Attach a band-aid below, or multiple ones if you wish. Write the name of people on or around it who are sick or in pain. Pray for them. Send them a note or call them to let them know you prayed for them.

Jeremiah 30:17 For I will restore health unto you, and I will heal you of your wounds, saith the Lord.

☐ Myself
☐ My family
☐ My church
☐ My community
☐ My world

Everyone has good days and bad days. God wants us to talk to Him about our feelings, our troubles, and even the things that make us happy. Use a crayon or pen color that best describes how you are feeling today, and write down your **thoughts, feelings, and anything that may be bothering you**. Pray about those things.

☐ Myself
☐ My family
☐ My church
☐ My community
☐ My world

Psalm 139:2 You know when I sit and when I rise; you perceive my thoughts from afar.

TAKE A WHIFF!

The Bible says that God created everything for His glory. Glue or tape a flower below.

Thank God for the beautiful **nature** that He created all around you. Draw other flowers or a scene to go with the flower you attached.

☐ Myself
☐ My family
☐ My church
☐ My community
☐ My world

Genesis 1:1 In the beginning God created the heavens and the earth.

Have someone else, such as a parent, teacher, pastor, or friend, write a prayer idea below, then do it!

 scripture goes here:

☐ Myself
☐ My family
☐ My church
☐ My community
☐ My world

Be a Scribe!

Many nations of the world are not fortunate to have a copy of the Bible, or one in their language. This makes it difficult for them to know about God. Copy a Bible chapter below. Pray that the Word of God would be **translated** into all the languages of the World and that Bibles would be allowed in the nations.

1 Timothy 2:3-4 This is good, and pleases God our Savior, who wants all men to be saved and to come to a knowledge of the truth.

- ☐ Myself
- ☐ My family
- ☐ My church
- ☐ My community
- ☐ My world

CHA-CHING!

Jesus told us that we shouldn't use money foolishly. How do you or your family spend money? Tape a bill, grocery, clothes, gas, or other receipt from something your family has spent **money** on recently. Ask God to continue to provide your needs and help each of you to spend your money wisely.
Write your prayer below.

☐ Myself
☐ My family
☐ My church
☐ My community
☐ My world

1 Timothy 6:10 For the love of money is the root of all evil...

kidsprayer.com

Sowing Seed

The Bible teaches us that what we do (we plant) comes back to us (we reap.) If we are kind, we get kindness back. Tape a seed below (or several) and write down what kind of seed it is. Pray that you would plant good "**seeds of kindness and love**" around you, where they will grow to good relationships. Using the seed(s) below, draw a picture of your seeds sprouting into plants.

☐ Myself
☐ My family
☐ My church
☐ My community
☐ My world

Galatians 6:7 whatever one sows, that will he also reap...

kidsprayer.com

MINTY MOUTHS

God doesn't like bad words, lies, gossip, or talking bad about others. Smear toothpaste below (you can even make designs in it.) Ask God to help you remember to say **good things** about others, **not** to lie, and to have **clean conversations**. Write your prayer around your design after it dries.

☐ Myself
☐ My family
☐ My church
☐ My community
☐ My world

Ephesians 4:29 Let no corrupt communication proceed out of your mouth, but that which is good to the use of edifying, that it may minister grace unto the hearers.

Treasure Hunt

People who don't know God must be shown or told how to find or know Him. Hide an item somewhere where a friend can find it. Draw a treasure map with clues for them to use. Ask God to help you tell others how to find out more about Him. Pray that He would send more **missionaries** to nations who need them to tell them about Him.

Matthew 7:7 Ask and it will be given to you; seek and you will find; knock and the door will be opened to you.

- ☐ Myself
- ☐ My family
- ☐ My church
- ☐ My community
- ☐ My world

kidsprayer.com

Bound Buddies

God doesn't wants anyone to be alone; we all need friends. Tie two items together and attach to the page below. This could be shoe strings, spaghetti noodles, yarn, rubber bands, etc. One item represents you and the other represents a friend. Pray that you would be the **best friend** you can be, and that you will **listen** to them, and **love** them. Write your prayer around the items.

☐ Myself
☐ My family
☐ My church
☐ My community
☐ My world

Ecclesiastes 4:12 A person standing alone can be attacked and defeated, but two can stand back-to-back and conquer. Three are even better, for a triple-braided cord is not easily broken.

Squeaky Clean

Are you spiritually clean today? Or have you had **bad feelings** or said **bad things** about someone? Have you **lied, cheated**, had a **bad attitude** at home, or **disobeyed a parent or leader** over you? If you have, write a prayer of **repentance** below, then pray it. Don't feel bad when you are done repenting, just thank God that **He has forgiven you** and made your heart clean.

Psalm 51:10 Create in me a clean heart, O God; and renew a right spirit within me.

- ☐ Myself
- ☐ My family
- ☐ My church
- ☐ My community
- ☐ My world

Disaster Recipe

Without directions or rules our world and everything around us would be a mess. Write a recipe below, then **mark out one item or one instruction step**. How do you think the food would look or taste without it. **Ask God to help you follow** His directions for your life, those in the Bible, and those from your parents and leaders.

☐ Myself
☐ My family
☐ My church
☐ My community
☐ My world

John 14:23 Jesus replied, "All who love me will do what I say...

kidsprayer.com

Pet Pals

Everyone needs a pal, no matter how old or how young they are. Glue or tape some dry dog or cat food below. Write a prayer for those who are **lonely**, especially the elderly who often wish for companionship such as a pet.

☐ Myself
☐ My family
☐ My church
☐ My community
☐ My world

Hebrews 13:5 ...I will never leave you nor forsake you.

kidsprayer.com

YOUR iDEA GOES HERE

Have someone else, such as a parent, teacher, pastor, or friend, write a prayer idea below, then do it!

scripture goes here:

☐ Myself
☐ My family
☐ My church
☐ My community
☐ My world

kidsprayer.com

HUNGRY?

You probably didn't worry if you were going to eat today, but many people of the world did. Bite the edges of this page. How does it taste? Pray for those who are **hungry** and thirsty that God would provide **food, water and shelter** for them. Write your prayer below.

Matthew 5:6 God blesses those who hunger and thirst for justice, for they will be satisfied.

- ☐ Myself
- ☐ My family
- ☐ My church
- ☐ My community
- ☐ My world

Greased Up

Fathers have a lot of **responsibility** at work and at home. They need prayer and **support** from their family. Smear grease or oil from a tool or vehicle below. Write a prayer for your father, grandfather, or other fatherly person in your life, then pray it.

☐ Myself
☐ My family
☐ My church
☐ My community
☐ My world

Proverbs 23:22 Listen to your father, who gave you life, and don't despise your mother when she is old.

Mini Hopscotch

Families have lots of needs and **you can make a difference**. Draw a hopscotch drawing below. In each square, write a prayer request regarding your family or family members. Using a tiny pebble, uncooked rice, bead or other tiny item, roll it into the drawing. Pray the request listed in the box you land in. Continue to play until all squares have been prayed over.

☐ Myself
☐ My family
☐ My church
☐ My community
☐ My world

James 5:16 ...The prayer of a righteous person has great power as it is working.

kidsprayer.com

Coupon Prayer

We need to be willing to pray for others whenever they have a need; it's not just our needs that we should pray about. Make a **FREE PRAYER** coupon on another piece of paper. Give it to someone and tell them they can use it whenever they wish. When they use the coupon, pray for whatever need they have and paste the coupon below. Write down what you prayed for.

☐ Myself
☐ My family
☐ My church
☐ My community
☐ My world

Philippians 2:4 Do not merely look out for your own personal interests, but also for the interests of others.

kidsprayer.com

Pretty & Perfumed

Mothers are busy people. They take care of their family, their home, other people, and sometimes a job. Spray perfume from your mother, grandmother, or other motherly person in your life. Write a prayer for her below. Pray that she would have a **sweet**, **loving** spirit, and that God would use her to help those who are around her and to take care of her family.

☐ Myself
☐ My family
☐ My church
☐ My community
☐ My world

Proverbs 31:28 Her children stand and bless her. Her husband praises her...

Somewhere, over the ...

Have you ever had someone break a promise they made to you? It doesn't feel good. Draw and color a rainbow below. Write down some promises you've made to others or God. Thank God for keeping His promise to not destroy the Earth again by a **flood**. Ask Him to remind you to keep **promises** that you've made. If you haven't repent, and try to.

☐ Myself
☐ My family
☐ My church
☐ My community
☐ My world

Matthew 5:33 Again, you have heard that it was said to the people long ago, 'Do not break your oath, but keep the oaths you have made to the Lord...

kidsprayer.com

WHO AM I?

God made you unique and special, just as you are. You don't have to be popular, athletic, look like a supermodel or be a star to be special. Paste a picture of a model (if you are a girl) or a sports start (if you are a guy.) Put a **big black X** through the picture. Write down what you think God likes about you. Pray that you would be who God wants you to be, and not who everyone else thinks or says you should be.

Jeremiah 1:5 I knew you before I formed you in your mother's womb. Before you were born I set you apart and appointed you as my prophet to the nations.

- ☐ Myself
- ☐ My family
- ☐ My church
- ☐ My community
- ☐ My world

With this Ring...

Marriage can be tough sometimes. Every married person needs **God's strength** and **wisdom** to have a good relationship. Draw or make two rings out of paper, foil, or something similar, and paste them below. Write the names of two people who are married to each other next to the rings. Pray for their marriage.

☐ Myself
☐ My family
☐ My church
☐ My community
☐ My world

Genesis 2:18 And the Lord God said, It is not good that the man should be alone; I will make him an help meet for him.

 Schoolwork, Yuk!

The Bible tells us that one of the greatest things we can ever have is wisdom and knowledge. Tape or glue a graded school paper below. Pray that God would help you to **learn, understand, and remember** what you are learning. You may wish to paste a friend's graded paper instead, especially if they really need some help! Write your prayer below.

James 1:5 If you need wisdom, ask our generous God, and he will give it to you. He will not rebuke you for asking.

☐ Myself
☐ My family
☐ My church
☐ My community
☐ My world

kidsprayer.com

Quit Bugging Me!

Can you imagine having bugs for food instead of bread, grain, or vegetables? Some nations have this problem because bugs each their crops. Glue a dead bug or bugs below. Pray for those areas of the world where **plagues, diseases, and bugs** destroy crops and people's food. Write your prayer around the bug(s).

- ☐ Myself
- ☐ My family
- ☐ My church
- ☐ My community
- ☐ My world

Philippians 4:19 And this same God who takes care of me will supply all your needs from his glorious riches, which have been given to us in Christ Jesus.

Sincerely Yours

God loves your worship and praise. It doesn't matter if you are guy or girl, He wants to know what you think of Him. Write a **gushy**, love note to God below, then read it to Him.

Luke 10:27 ...You must love the LORD your God with all your heart, all your soul, all your strength, and all your mind...

- ☐ Myself
- ☐ My family
- ☐ My church
- ☐ My community
- ☐ My world

kidsprayer.com

La la la la la....

Maybe you aren't a rock star or a famous singer, but when you sing and worship God, it gets His attention and He listens.

Write your own **song** about God or to God below. Sing it to Him and share it with someone else, if you wish.

☐ Myself
☐ My family
☐ My church
☐ My community
☐ My world

Ephesians 5:19 singing psalms and hymns and spiritual songs among yourselves, and making music to the Lord in your hearts...

WHAT ABOUT ME?

It's easy to take our family for granted; we are used to them always being around. But many children don't have a family, and they are very lonely. Paste a picture of your family (or draw a picture of them) below. Pray for all the **orphans** of the world who don't have a loving, Christian family. Cut out a paper doll kid and add to your family to represent them finding a **Christian** family. Give them a name. Pray that your own family would grow closer together.

Psalm 68:5 Father to the fatherless, defender of widows--this is God, whose dwelling is holy.

☐ Myself
☐ My family
☐ My church
☐ My community
☐ My world

kidsprayer.com

Have someone else, such as a parent, teacher, pastor, or friend, write a prayer idea below, then do it!

scripture goes here:

☐ Myself
☐ My family
☐ My church
☐ My community
☐ My world

YOUR iDEA GOES HERE

Have someone else, such as a parent, teacher, pastor, or friend, write a prayer idea below, then do it!

 scripture goes here:

- ☐ Myself
- ☐ My family
- ☐ My church
- ☐ My community
- ☐ My world

kidsprayer.com

YOUR IDEA GOES HERE

Have someone else, such as a parent, teacher, pastor, or friend, write a prayer idea below, then do it!

scripture goes here:

- ☐ Myself
- ☐ My family
- ☐ My church
- ☐ My community
- ☐ My world

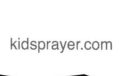

YOUR IDEA GOES HERE

Have someone else, such as a parent, teacher, pastor, or friend, write a prayer idea below, then do it!

 scripture goes here:

☐ Myself
☐ My family
☐ My church
☐ My community
☐ My world

Made in the USA
Middletown, DE
16 March 2022

62725514R00055